Are You Listening?

by

M. Stutterheim

Copyright © 2020 All rights reserved.

No part of this publication may be produced or stored in or introduced into a retrieval system or transmitted in any form without prior permission of author
(e-mail contact: countryplacebb@yahoo.com).

Cover Design: L S
Photos Design: MMAS
ISBN   978-0-9895511-7-5

Printed in the United States of America

Collection of Poetry & Brief Prose

Dedicated to my thirteen siblings

Contents

Introduction..1

The Lover..3
Miraculous...4
The COVID Chapel....................................5
PHOTO...6
Pointed Finger...7
Cells...8
Momentous..9
A Man's View..10
Suffocation...11
Forty Years Ago..12
Hesitating...13
Hydatidiform mole..................................14
Forgiveness..15
Adoption..16
The Recital...17
Beautiful...18
Rescue Pilot...19
Vibrant One...20
True Measure..21
PHOTO...22
Friendship..23
Wooden Box..24
Aggression...25
Distance..26

Turned On..27
The Evidence..28,29
Cats and Kids...30,31
Her Day...32
The Preacher Said..33
Too Much..34
Noise...35
Enlightenment 40 + The Heart of It All........36,37
Gardens..38,39
PHOTO...40
Motion..41
Consider This..42
I'm So Proud...43
Rightful Place...44
Blessed...45
Diverge or Amuse..46,47
A Battle + Desire..48
Something I'm Not...49
The Body..50
In the Game...51
Hugs and Embraces...52
Do You Understand?...53
PHOTO...54
Trembling Birthday...55
Selfless Man...56
Footprint...57
Old Woman..58
Lost Minds...59
The Hand + My Excuse....................................60,61

The Papa Prayer..62,63
A Night Out..64
After...65
Suffering Explained..66
One View + Another View......................................67
To Lie..68
You Hurt So Beautifully..69
I AM...70
Aging Sexuality...71
PHOTO..72
The Forest Rap...73
Inviting Risk..74
To Another...75
Girl of Multiplicity...76
What Happened?..77
Red Love..78
The Young Man and His Dog................................79
The Poet's Response to the Student.....................80
COVID unmasked..81
She is Strong..82
The Tease..83
Faithful...84
President's Day + Saints and Warriors............85
PHOTO...86
The Chief..87
Good-bye?..88
The Visit...89
Boomerang...90
All Occasions...91

Generations	92
A Different Way	93
Heat	94
An Example of Love	95
Today	96
Wall	97
PHOTO	98
Who Am I?	99
To be a Saint	100
Not of the World	101
The Cross	102
Just Once	103
Utopia	104
A Future	105
My Gut Feeling	106
Again	107
Discussion	109

Introduction

When I was a stranger on the Big Red Island in the middle of the great waters, I adapted to a new channel of communicating. And now, I ask the reader to do the same. "Are you listening?" Without academic or technical prosody, this is my poetic language—a small wave of extraordinaire! Will it provoke unique emotion, and emotions of universal commonality; your ear will be the judge. I hope my lines will validate you—like a stranger acclimated. So to the reader, I offer this possibility. Thank you for listening!

—Marie Stutterheim

The Lover

My life shortens when I'm with you

Those brief words of revelation
By the lover who loves himself
To the first who becomes second

Being naive and infatuated with ideas
The phrase baffles and excites her

But not beyond a third or fourth hour
Only for the strangest moment of elevation
When he chose not to elaborate

Yet life ought to have skipped dates
Had disclosure been sought, and

Negated the fifth dimension

Miraculous

It was 5:00 am.

Stillness awakened,
Several seconds, several minutes,
Stillness hugged and kept me calm.
If this was the end, I was okay —
No words, no pain, no buzzing in my head;
I welcomed it, until it shocked
And stillness shattered
With, "I love you."

A voice,
No shape, no body, but immense and gentle,
Then gone.
It was sad, lovely, and never again.
The quiet, the miracle, the comforting voice;
If I spoke of it, who would believe —
The risk scolded, "Bury it now"
Until that day...

Only to him
It was revealed;
And goodness
Held, and hugged me closer.

The COVID Chapel

No longer barred from seeking consolation, the unlocked door opened my eyes to stark clean: barren pews and stiff flowers speaking of vacuity occupied
— AND YET — the central altar, devoid of décor, supported a cross, a large book, a white cloth, and an empty vessel of yesterday and tomorrow
— AND THUS — I rested my human impression upon the cushioned kneeler, to declare a prayer to be said, but nothingness entered my head
— AND SO — in the quiet, I rose to illuminate a blue votive, only to peer into its nonexistence of wax and wicker that had no power to melt my aloneness away.

Pointed Finger

In the garden,
Man pointed his finger with shallow defense.
Written words regulate hence...
Centuries of ideology

Suppositions;
More pointed fingers, at the woman of course
Standing by man without remorse...
Centuries of misinterpretation

Bring her down.
Pointed fingers of ultimate fall,
With her exploration, her wisdom stalled...
Centuries of indenture

Ultimately,
A pointed finger
Like a loaded gun
Emitted control;
And centuries continued...

Cells

Multiplying
with intention
some rejected
some succeeding
creating
though bursting
perfect or deformed
yet attached

Examine now
the legal
the factual
the difficult
problematic
questions escalating
decision making
too harsh

Cells attached
in limbo
experimenting
amazing
frightening
while you propose
choice
by your definition

Momentous

I'm here trying to grasp
what is
most important.

Mo — Missouri — here I am
and this thought
presses ominous,
large and looming of

Men — uniformed,
threatening; and
I'm feeling distraught

To
regard this
or any action
or any symbol that eradicates

Us — the other,
as we stand
angry or small
or terribly splintered.

Mo-men-to-us.

That's why — I'm here
grasping
what's most important.

A Man's View

I stayed
to prove my point:
the framed can be tamed.

The trap is presented,
innately ingrained.

Smooth nose,
alert ears, no fears,
now relaxed, leaning close.

My lead, beastly greed,
the hunger pull,
and nothing dull.

She is tense, self-defense;
and who will win?

Suffocation

You love me so much I could drink
You suffocate and make me sink

There is much more, can't you see
I make this weary, weary plea

Don't possess me with your beer
Don't hold me and call me dear

There's a reason for this to end
If you'll wise up and not resent

My time alone

Forty Years Ago

"Let's change the station."

That's why he would remember
the side by side
and yet fatigued by the holiday music,
fatigued with truth, grace, righteousness and love,
all condensed in one stanza.

He always struggled with Christmas
for joy and pain were inseparable;
even now,
while staring at her
he remembered the side by side
and avoiding the outer world of
lies, manipulation, injustice and hate...
aware that hope died
with not wanting fatherhood, when it
seemed most likely.

"You will change," she had said.

It was forty years ago
and he had wiped the moist brow,
wiped her laboring face, and stepped back
and prayed for compassion
to enter her committed soul;
and for a brief moment
he was birthing their child
and apprehension left,
and the cry arrived
with such ecstasy — side by side.

Hesitating

I want to call
But I don't
Nothing to do with anxiety or stress
But I can't quite put my finger on it... I hesitate

I want to call
But I don't
Nothing to do with punishment or pain
But I do believe it can be traced... I hesitate

I want to call
But I don't
This has something to do
With enlightenment... I hesitate

I want to call
But I don't
As you'll tire of me
Is that fair? No. I hesitate

I want to call
And I may
Nothing to do with you
And all the others, just me, hesitating

Hydatidiform mole

Just silence and more silence
    as deformity allows
        without heart or kindness
    or any beat of
        shared existence

Silence and more silence
    nine months
        within a womb
    as clusters of fluid cells
        until effort brings forth

        no life

Forgiveness

Audacity believes
that forgiveness is
offered only
at *our* appointed time—
yet conscience will say
that's wrong, as
forgiveness is the moment
of God's grace.

Inflicted pain
hardens the heart;
but discernment
does not blame *the other*;
instead, we will understand
that our projection
is destructive or futile,
and basically not fair.

Now consider
lack of communication,
unintended reaction,
or misinterpretation of neglect.
If you and *the other* have value,
pray beyond expectation,
and forgiveness
will occur.

Adoption

The longest lashes
Lamenting eyes
The dark and light
Missing him

The fingering frown
Around and around
The lingering
Missing her

The gifted road
Laboring lucent
The loveliest smiles
Missing no one

Donnie and Miranda
Adopted

The Recital

A shy and silent man
Adjusts his meager space,
A cause for all to ponder —
Fate now seats a place.

A bent gesture forward
Predicts a gently pause;
Position takes the firm,
And hint of caution falls.

With long fingers gliding
Over ivory key release,
To marry sweetest chords —
Oh! Sound of lovely ease!

The magic on the stage
Hastens our lifted praise,
Testing near and yonder
In classic wonder plays.

No longer shy and silent
Among the grandest hall,
The tension is dismissed
By music man and all.

Beautiful

She met him only twice
Inches taller than her five foot five
Firm, well built, and shaven head
But what struck her deeply was his aura of serenity
He had lived longer than her
And yet no audacious words uttered from his lips
No reflective theory on life
No long discourse
Nor words of wisdom to guide her youth
In any particular direction

But something noble and true
Was present in this soldier
He had survived situations
And had discovered something profound
Still, not daring to share
The unduplicated
And when she read his note
Writing "true measure"
Relating to a width, and depth of life
So vague, she sighed

Had she expected more...
He left a beautiful book, a gift so rare
And when winter arrived
She felt his presence
In pages aware

Rescue Pilot

there is a man in the shadows of heart
behind hovering clouds, with proven start
passing each beach, rallied in air
and checking his data with detailed care
and damage is read via signaled lines
as floaters toss with no living signs
like breathless below, on deep ocean floor
a drowning proof far from the shore

each tormented search, battles with wind
knowing time terrors the weathered fin
as rendered service distresses to see
real evidence burned among black debris
yet desperate yearns for lives returned
but repeated effort marks gutted churn
for the man of mission, enlisted in part
sees no rescue for the shadowed heart

The Vibrant One

Like the seasonal change in an autumn maple
She is bold, resistant, adorning color
Like a shadow growing over distraught lawns
She is posturing, curious, overwhelming
Like the sun striking a shallow water pool
She is heated, intense, stubbornly cleansing
Like a breeze passing through the narrow gate
She is carrying her self, and blowing the rest
Like the path breathing a point over and over
She is creating cause and leaving her history
Like a destination, she inspires — but then
She marches off in another direction

True Measure

If life is measured by length,
width and depth define
the person.

If love is measured by oneness,
differences reflect our God.

If rule is measured by domain,
independence seeks freedom.

If the future is measured by science,
tomorrow will plague
you and me.

Friendship

Asking little
Takes up
Where it leaves off

Casual defines
His place or mine
He chuckles, we sit

He takes my hand
Tucks it warm
Like morning

Lips move
With sweetness
In reviews, in twos

Affection
No strings
Nor knots

Wooden Box

Deception
Bold and sold
Brokered five
Traffic told
Battered youth
Some will die
Stormy seas
Hidden nigh
Famished weak
Bodies reek
Ship to shore
None to seek
Branding tow
Under stow
Like an old
Wooden box

Aggression

Beyond the dry
Dividing brush
The cave invaded
Curses deep
A desert thirst
Of chamber thrill

Wildness thrust
Its form and rise
Like blowing dunes
Until repeats
Soon exhaust
Abrasive heaves

Beware, beware
A cave invaded
Lies not quiet
Neither still
Of dessert thrill
And thirst for more

Distance

They sat
A whisper away
Testing
One sought less
Another sought trust
Eventually
Sensual would offend
The mind embodied

Even while
Listening
Facts defined
A silence
Depriving
Possibilities
If life should be
Too dull

Turned On

I am passionate about my dictionary.
It stimulates — and arouses me.

I find a word,
or words.
My mind is turned on
with fortunate vitality,
possessing most ardently
endless realms —
provoking obsession,
until I burst!

Words
beyond substance.

The Evidence

There had to be proof.
I was hell bent on locating it.
Palpitations,
breathing slowly, again and again,
"Heaven help me, St. Anthony."
It works every time —
thump, thump — today a bit longer.
"It's okay," to myself, I say,
and dump the coffee
and calmly phone.

"Could you look for it?"
"I'll try, when I get back."
"Where are you going?"
"California..."

I have other sisters. Six possibilities.
They could possess it.
But I shouldn't make a spectacle of myself.
So who else? It must be found.
I scroll 5001 pictures on the I-Phone,
and tire myself.

Back to the file container — the second time;
then back to twelve albums
and the search continues
for the instamatic,
three by five,
photos and more photos.
I scatter sixty-eight years of my life
over the rug; no luck.
And now?
Ask auntie.

She is the world's best memory keeper—
an eighty-eight year old semi-invalid woman.
"May I come over?" I admit my intent.
She was receptive.
After fifty-five minutes, the evidence is located.
She adds, "Of course, it's important."

The black and white photo:
City backdrop. A porch. Steps.
The pretty woman on the right
is holding a bundle.
Another to the left
has a boy beside him.
The third — the significant —
has dark wavy hair,
a movie star mustache,
and looks brazenly amused.
Three young sons
surround him,
and there I am,
a chubby child
sitting on his lap,
my moment
of importance.
Evidence.

Cats and Kids

litter three for the gray stray mama
he threatens again, to take them away
we, the kids, behind a door
shrivel, as anxiety
           attacks the room

she cries as if they are babies
yet his words grow vehement
our instinct says, do not move
and we listen, intensely
           with hidden faces

her sob suffers foreboding
his stomping is severe
he leaves the house, leaves us trembling
of fate bundled
           and squirming

that memory too often repeated
a projection of cats to kids
about the expendable
if parents should demand
           a riddance

can the human mother birth a surplus
in the same strain, it fatigues the father
and this diminishes attachments
and lessen the worth
           of extras

questions flood the psyche
this survival of fit or favored
among populations exposed
in expectation that the weak
              won't live

cats and kids are not far apart
when basic value is discarded
voiding numbered spirits
like the litter disposed —
              gunny-sacked....

        drowning in the pond

Her Day

Caffeine, a chipped mug
how I do worry
about her day
padded surround
mandated safety
so controlled
now weaker
than coffee with cream
gone
the nettling
the aggravations
puckering
her dry lips
she's trapped
in transparent flesh
like naked in a nest
self-neglect
anti-social
without effort
bruised badly
in withdrawal
but oh
may I interrupt
and swoop her
under my wing
back to participation
yet I shudder
and sip slowly
in the middle of May

The Preacher Said

For a brief moment
Or a long duration
Examine
Communication
Between
The unfriendly

Superficial
Meanness, not intended
Infliction is interpreted
Before
Transference
Is made

But when enlightened
In other shoes
In other eyes
Empathy grows
And before long
Peace

Too Much

Fatigue hits me hard
I can't think—I can't speak
Beats and blows
If such continues
My mind
May shatter
Like a drum
Thrown hard
Against a wall

Noise

My ears
Ringing, screaming
It never departs
In desperation
I imagine this the voice of angels
But then
Heaven would be hell
So I choose petition
Pleading prayer
Voices of the unknown
Crying out
For intercession
And then, only then, the ringing has a purpose
If I can bear it
I shall hope
To lighten my pain
If not, the screaming has no end

And I will join the dead

Enlightenment 40

When they bore their own
I was amputated
Not in a physical way
But psychologically
Due to a sense
Of their *own* motherhood
Yet a stub remains
As their parenthood
Reminds them
That affinity is strong

Circumstances
Do differ
But the heart is similar
As the goal is presented
For each generation
To create tools for betterment
Maintaining ties
Until severance is possible
And yet, impossible
Because of kinship

Ultimately, they do understand
Well, perhaps not
Because their duties
Remain mixed
While mimicking our stories
Though that is the *last thing*
They wish to hear
So in the discourse
We listen
And they talk

Still opportunity is lost
To benefit from the past
And since pride is important
Progress may be hindered
But not always
As they are women
With breakthroughs
And enlightenment
That speaks to the souls
As daughters to mother

The Heart of It All

Like the *actor* proclaiming love
Or the writer extolling *craft*
You cheer me
Without the heart
Of a passionate soul

Gardens

I went to the library years ago and picked up a book called *The One Hour Garden, No Fuss, No Work,* and of course I checked it out.

The one-hour-garden. You plan it, you create it, you enjoy it, maintain it... No fuss, no work? You water it, you weed it, you mulch it, and even sweet-talk the tulips, crocus, daffodils, columbines, peonies, coral bell, daylilies, pansies, lavenders, irises, bachelor buttons, petunias, crocus, and baby's breath.

When friends stopped by, we would sip a small glass of wine together on the back of the deck, and discuss the latest floral delights, and the newest hybrids, and the grand display of seasonal colors.

When the unexpected dropped by, we would rock back and forth on the porch swing, and talk about the weather and this creation while offering them a connection to the garden.

Then one rainy Saturday, I explored a large outlet and saw something called *God's Wonderful Creation*. I bought it. The book was all about butterflies, which are such delightful creatures.

Not long after, I observed fifty some species fluttering playfully from one flower to the next. This gave me new pleasure and there was balance in my garden and my life.

Years passed. I felt an ache here and there and eventually that turned into full blooming arthritis: back hurt, knees hurt, and I felt irritable all over. Even small physical exertions were too much!

After a bout with gout, I looked at my garden and its fourteen flower varieties, and suddenly, they represented pain. A thought entered my head: maybe I should remove one or two or three. Less fuss. Less work. My balance may return.

Not so. Butterflies started to disappear...

So another decision: I called in for assistance and replanted the three lost varieties. My beautiful garden was whole again.

Then I hired a daily worker. It was simple. And now the pleasure is back, and so are the butterflies — a hundred or more.

Motion

moving along
pushing ahead
the whitest skin
full of moisture
a broader sweep
over surface
until it feels
the first long curve
so deep and full
taken easy
laying aside
interruptions
another round
a smooth motion
nothing resists
the yellow blade
of father's Ford
never faltering
in love with snow
moving along

Consider This

Machines need not define him
Competing, planning, tuning
The irrational stout
Tinkering, toying, ejecting
Until it sputters a pout

Machines need not resign him
Resting, wasting, shrinking
Which cast a serious doubt
Denying, lying, defying
That masculine peters out

Machines need not deface him
Testing, receiving, settling
A rational takes new route
Renewing, designing, seeing
Position remedies clout

Machines will never replace him
His being daring, waiting
For peers of power about
Questing, sighting, believing
A winning rise to shout

I'm So Proud

At first he said, just go away
Her firm position and bold eyes
Earnest from every angle
Was feistier than he could fathom

Up against a tigress
In the local habitat
Movements methodical
Deliberate, convincing
Unrelenting
Never go away
I'm so proud
She'll stay

Rightful Place

One woman
Pedestal
Nearly divine

    One woman
    Prayerful
    Noted Jewish

One woman
Positioned
Never weary

    One woman
    Predestined
    Known as fact

Other women
Pluralistic
Narrating

    One woman
    Promoting
    Nerving others

All women
Placed in
Nodding Status

Blessed

Oh blessed art thou
You say to her
The virgin one
Singularly
    What you mean
    Is worse than bad
    Erasing — us
    So subtly
Since blessed is she
Demands unique
A worthy status
Miraculously
    What you preach
    Empowers — you
    Reduces us
    So readily
Oh blessed are they
A grace more true
Lift the women
Plural-ly
    Thou shall create
    The world anew
    That presses us
    Equally
Blessed art thou
Blessed art they
Ask what it is
Test the inclusive

Diverge or Amuse

Pacified sex
Paper profit
Pajama days
Pampered wives
Papal nuns
Pardoned crime
Passionate hermit
Patient coach
Patriarchal Christian
Pawning risk
Pectoral tits
Pennywise spenders
Perforated protection
Perilous dreams
Perspective art
Perverse good
Pilfering banker
Pitiful rich
Pleasing cemetery
Plucky coward
Polite politician
Porky dietician
Portable outhouse
Positive negative
Powerless thorn
Praying Mantis
Preachy sinner
Precarious grace
Precocious doll
Preferable pain
Pre-ordained walls
Prestigious pharmacy
Preserved aging

Presumptuous husbands
Priceless love
Privileged orphan
Procrastinating winner
Progressive autocrat
Promiscuous penguin
Prophetic end
Protective boss
Provocative purity
Psycho saint
Public secrets
Purging prison
Puzzling epiphany

A Battle

A jillion weeds
Surround the seeds
My reaching claws
On legs and paws
Attack the green
Of roots unseen
To sprout again
Like men and war

Desire

I want red and passion
small budding
tugs my side

She climbs, in some fashion
and pricks me
open wide

Sun will spread a ration
as she kisses
petal pride

Yet she voids my passion
and yellow
claims a bride

Something I'm Not

Hair, an amazing thing
it creates an identity
that can be changed on a whim, if
I have the money, and time, to sit in an elevated chair
like royalty, for forty minutes — or perhaps
for two hours — to have someone listen to my day
or chatter on about clients before me
or extend the local gossip, or
choose the oddest topic
because the seat is mine
and meanwhile, the other takes instruction
and turns me into someone I hardly recognize

So when I slide off the throne
and check my view for the umpteenth time
to have magnified myself in this new look
oh my, the bill and the tip is enough to erase
a return next month, or even next year
yet it won't be long, and someone and the color
will make my hair red, or even crazy pink
or make it kinky, or keep it straight
quite sure the phenomenal exist
that I can be easily transformed
to become something I'm not
and the fantasy will carry on!

The Body

Cumbersome and large
with a mind

that assesses
your weight

You reject me
and hide me
in a closet

One sixty
one eighty
two hundred and rising
and rising
and rising

The heavy
has no relief
as my number

registers
your disbelief

with a
commercial scale

In the Game

My hand is there
Callous rough
Abrasive wear

My heart is old
No less tough
That I'm told

My head is hard
Without her
Just play a card

My hope is thin
Not alone
Just pass the gin

My hell is real
No big deal

Hugs and Embraces

The "how's all going" shoulder embrace, answers
the inquisitive.

The "thank-you" exit embrace reinforces secure departure.

The tiny tot hug that encircles the knees mellows
the shy inside.

The handshake embrace, settles the sure and firm.

The fearful hug admits a worrisome delay of serious routes.

The "I love you" embrace, with hesitation, may set the stage
for further exploration.

The double snug hug, approached from right and left,
squeezes the sensibilities.

The caressing embrace, stirs imagery more rapid
than rain in spring.

The celebration hug is supplemented with
noise and laughter.

The "been awhile" embrace sorts fuzzy from sad,
and healing begins.

The no touch, six-foot space, pantomimed hug, accepts the
persistent COVID.

Do You Understand?

I don't want to be special

Specifically different
Patented as peculiar
Not belonging
Identity critiqued
An unusual species

I want to be normal

Socially accepted
Regular sort
Mentally stable
Average intelligence
Loved, simply loved

I want to be — me

Trembling Birthday

Holy crap!
The car has died.

Meters from the track,
I get out and lift the hood
to analyze the motor,
not aware I've run out of gas.
You see, the *anticipation of sixteen*
has made attentiveness ridiculous.

At this moment
fuel is irrelevant
in that the distant quiet
is turning to rumble —
soon trembling will be obvious,
as the coal train rolls
closer and closer,
and I stand undecided.

I ignore the train. Dang!
Do I trust my evolving?
With stupor to movement,
the question disappears
beyond the noisy iron rails
as my cell catches a signal,
with pulse in pocket coming to life
and help on the way!!!

Sixteen goes on...

Selfless Man

You grace us with another generation.
You offer guidance to the young rising.
You cherish a location that binds our lives.
You widen horizons to be a healing instrument.
You risk the unknown of multiple disruptions.
You follow a mission with ardent sacrifice.
You smile with pondering thoughts.
You love with the kindest affection.
You model the selfless man.

His Footprint

He entered through persuasion
with a history unto himself.
Lineage had confused his name, yet
patience waited the unfolding
of a revelation among
generations.

As he trusted loyalties,
doors were painted blue and green
and windows opened full and wide
with the warmest radiating
his gifts with magical moments
to enlighten.

With disclosure and a marvelous note,
this man marked his path and more
leaving a footprint of humor,
of creativity and support
that logged his journey
and all that belonged.

Old Woman

Her age is obvious.
Her mind plays tricks
Upon near and far,
Expecting acceptance,
And still believing
Unfair will erase
The late stage.

She denies progress.
She talks of loss,
Rejects endurance,
Diminishes self,
And reality hurts
As we can't erase
This stage.

Her apprehension,
Her proof
Holds paranoia,
Ruining assurance
Of tomorrow;
And no one can erase
What we know as
The end stage.

Lost Minds

morning half past
tea is cold
four closed walls
ghastly mold
the ghost is gone
the door left wide
nothing moves
even outside

table is set
chair sits by
still confused
the floor and I
in the corner
the rat is dead
under the wire
without a head

two lost minds

The Hand

The corridor, the long hall
      presents on the wall
every contortion, every line
that attempts to define
both dramatic and dim
      of the remarkable limb,

the hand, the photo,
reflects—him.

Masculine wrought,
      the photographer seeks
to sharply commit
a mesmerized fit
and render delay with
      the art of display—

I pause,
and so what do I see?

That rugged grip
      beyond the hip,
that paternal psyche
ready to strike
against deviation;
      it sets confrontation

with eternal sternness,
and forces a kiss.

The image supplies
      in a frame not wide,
the hand on the wall
that loaded gall:
the remarkable limb,
      a limb so grim

You.
No, no — it can't be.

My Excuse

Gadder
Nail it to a ladder

Roaming words
That may not matter
Are like tatter

With pit or patter
Frankly speaking
It's not my fiction

The Papa Prayer

It's both comforting and controversial
because *"Our Father"* may not connect
with the small beggar in South America,
with the abused orphan of Asia,
with the hungry masses of Africa.

Birth is a defined moment.
Life lacks reverence.

"Who art in heaven"; what is heaven —
A child's question and an adult's void
if there's no foundation of real place,
if there's no experience of community,
if there's no path toward secure faith.

Images bear nothing
When identity is hidden.

"Hallowed be thy name"; what is holy
for the neglected, the lost, the indigenous
without church support in Antarctica,
without land — the undesignated nation,
without protective services, as in Australia.

People are diluted and
Culture loses face.

"Thy Kingdom come, thy will be done";
Trust feel impossible for
the desolate within silent prisons,
the desperate within human trafficking,
the despondent within harsh migration.

Promises are false and
Words feed despair.

When Spirit is part of our lives,
"On earth, as it is, in heaven,"
it will shake the boundaries in Europe,
it will open the doors in North America,
it will increase hope in other lands.

We should open our eyes wide.
"Give us this day, our daily bread..."

A Night Out

Candles dim, so kind to my face
Are like dining wine

Silky scarfs, so kind to my grey
Are like wistful rhymes

Bluish beads, so kind to my breast
Are like dancing times

Pretty gloves, so kind to my hands
Are like covered signs

Weak sights
So kind to your eyes

After

Six *days ago,* he died
I knew him, and not his love

Six *hours ago,* she wilted
In the chair, in my den

Six *minutes ago,* she cried
Hiding that sodden smile

Six *seconds ago,* she replied
"But I'm happy"

And

Six *weeks, not more,* she'll deny
Memories

Six *months will project* – that I'll die
Not knowing her well

Suffering Explained

One tells this story
of a dead mouse
stuck in a Vaseline jar;
it was thirty-five degrees.
Generosity with friends
meant not enough
for the utility bill.
The winter promised
suffering
but never homelessness.
Did that help misery to mend?
Suffering is always hard
to explain.

First View

My tears won't heal,
only my heart...
My fears won't relieve,
only my mind...
My doubts don't agree,
only my soul...
My trials won't see,
only my love...
My fears won't accept,
only you will accept

Second View

My tears won't heal my heart.
My fears won't relieve my mind.
My doubts don't agree with my soul.
My trials won't see my love.
My fears won't accept you.

To Lie

I used to think he was teasing.
Eventually it wore me down.

The half-truths.
The omissions.
The weird trifles.
Would not truth be easier?
Perhaps not.
Am I to blame?

My reactions.
My suspicions.
I interrogate.
I don't inquire.
Lies or fire?
Maybe truth is not easy.

You Hurt So Beautifully

You hurt so beautifully
    when pride disintegrates
        and tears streak visually
as your admission of error
    comes to my attention

You hurt so beautifully
    when feedback feeds frankly
        of your shallow effort
withdrawn somewhat humbly
    like a stumbling contract

You hurt so beautifully
    as facts finally accentuate
        what is less understood
and listening shatters pity
    knowing there's more

You hurt so beautifully
    but it's not necessary

I AM

He says the body and mind are nothing,
only I AM is consciousness.

Dissect him; all organs are found;
but I AM is present—it is timeless.

Sight, touch, taste, hearing, smell—
parts of body and mind—or I AM.

Is this the last romance, or is it love?

Aging Sexuality

Does defeat heat the sheet
    when limp
    will not
    leap
Does dread form a head
    if tension
    makes
    the bed
Does past dull the grasp
    when bursts
    weaken
    fast
Does rest mean no less
    if function
    fails
    a crest
Does device simply rise
    when limit
    tells
    no lies
Does this appall
    when aging
  recalls

  possibilities

The Forest Rap

A month goes by
with wooded why
as movement shy
is crushed by tie
to cut and kill
and render still
as horrid blade
removes the shade
so roots shall die
devoid of cry.
No green to reap
leaves none to weep
or to redeem
against the team
of fools and foul
and all that plows
to seek the goal
and dig the hole
for human lies
that call it wise.
A year goes by
we still ask why
the moans and groans
so caught by drones
was met by tones
like deaf and stones
and yet we know
with none to slow
the strong will rise
and soon devise
a sacred plan for the forest.

Inviting Risk

It's a warm process
      called closeness;
the phone text
is not the beam.

Can you tolerate
      basking fully
when exposure
would seem
more risky
than protective lotion,
for this would be
      to share a tan
without a text
between our souls!

To Another

You are confused as ants sprayed with rain.
You are vulnerable as a new berry bush.
You are droopy as daffodils wilting in spring.
You are unlocked as open wide shelter.

I am mindful as piercing fresh air.
I am hopeful as the wounded tree.
I am wishful as the potted seed.
I am retreating as the passing wind.

You are receptive as the clear blue sky.
You are thoughtful as blades of grass.
You are prepared as birds on a limb.
You are not stressed — for another day.

Girl of Multiplicity

I love the magnificence of the great cities,
but not the noise, the stench or congestion.
I treasure architecture and buildings—
the ornate, the grand, the historical,
and the modern reaching up
like mighty rockets for takeoff
from paved hard streets that accommodate.

I love the quiet of vast spaciousness,
but not the dirt, the dust, the harsh wind.
I enjoy the cottage and manors—
the small, the sprawling, the tidy farms with
light rays reaching broad
like invisible rakes combing the fields
as dry roads take me somewhere.

I love the convenience of smaller towns,
but not dogs, cats, or Sunday mowers.
I appreciate the neighborhood watch,
the children, the schools, the sports,
and the churches reaching out
like kindly good Samaritans
while brown brick streets welcome my stay.

What Happened?

Snow in November
Rain in December
January ice
February nice
March mask no more
April asks for sun
May ever blue
June dims dreary
July soulless dry
August reeks of rotten
Brown in September
Gone in October

Climate change

Red Love

It was not on the horizon
The blessed sun we know
And still you neglected me
In cheerless ten below

Oh how you ought to find me
Before the wind does flow
Your red throat should sing
And seek my chirp below

And now on the horizon
The rising moon of glow
And down you shall seek me
My weakened voice in tow

Oh how we ought to bond
Before the storm will grow
And rest with one another
Among the winter snow

The Young Man and His Dog

He rippled in like a wide brook; his young voice effeminate, his face round, and his dog *too beautiful*...

Then the burst, the starter, the odd statement "she's my lover," and brown and golden looked our way, soon to follow a scent to the front row, brushing our bended knees with less than brash curious sniffs, waiting for where and what and us — the seated audience, who were now stumped, and likely *bewildered*.

The young man beamed and proceeded with his presentation, weight on both feet, bugling again, "she's my lover" as the dog continued to be as alert as our own ears, and over and over we nudged each other, challenging "love" or "lover" between a four legged creature and the two legged companion — so *unusual*.

And yes, the young man and his dog won our attention.

The Poet's Response to the Student

who complains
it's *only* words
and not like music

who must whine
to make a song
not a poem

whatever, still listen

shorter, longer
thoughts and feeling
less or more

rhyme or no rhythm
and you'll find
a poem

and a song

COVID unmasked

I sweep the floor already clean
    I wash the table dirt unseen
I dust a frame against the grain
    I wipe the fear in the mirror
I cook the food to void a peril
    I rinse the dish three times sterile
I crave release without blame
    I walk the path part insane
I frown upon the barest face
    I see a risk with awful trace
I go back home now to groan
    I turn the dial and sit alone

She is Strong

I see her smile, near perfect teeth, streaked hair and painted nails, relaxing with wine — confident as the chef takes over.

I see her eyes during the meeting, professional eyes on the presenter, weighing the significant, each intonation and every gesture.

I see her faith in the church, left shoulder brushing softly against the dedicated spouse — she is committed to the kindest man.

I see her attempting a read amidst a game play, surrounded with thunder and lights, distracted by a novel, mystery or not.

I see her volunteering at a school project, stooping to assist the neglected child — offering specific aid, the necessary.

I see her energy in the berry patch, protected from thorny, collecting a large measure for consumption, or for share.

I see her sauntering in the park, surrounded with family, always forgiving crazy hurts — or whatever.

I see her sad spirit at the funeral, holding the white tissue, catching the first tears before the grief falls. And yet, she is strong.

The Tease

When I look into the glass
I see mother's aging face
Am I blessed or am I cursed
The glistening mirror could test

Once flawless full and cheerful pink
The sagging chin ask why
The wrinkles meet the frown between
The brow so set in rest

Now a grin, with eyes stretch thin
In effort I will try
To tease the mirror squarely dear
Like a playful pest

Faithful

I call
every Monday
when she's up.
"What's for lunch?"
"Food," she says.
"Having chili?"
"No, no, not cold."
A disconnect.
Not unusual.

I sense
some clarity
as she stalls,
and then admits,
"I walked today."
It's clear
he came by
for more than
warm chocolate.

"A walk is good."
"You think so."
And then contrary,
"I'm going to bed."
That concludes,
why she's tired
of him, of me.
Still, every Monday,
I call.

President's Day

The count came down
Let us weep

Red tolled up
Took a creep
Absent vote
Let it reap
Hacked polls
Dig deep

The count came down
Let us weep

Saints and Warriors

If sacrifice is coveted
for religion
and/or exhilaration
then life is
all screwed up

The Chief

The matrilineal line,
The matriarchal voice...

Don't mock and stalk me, you tribal foe
Don't map and trap me as winter doe
Don't bind the signs of horse and Crow

I'll rock the flock and pull the bow
I'll leap and keep in rain and snow
I'll hold the cold and summer stow

No walk and talk to ride the flow
No stake and rake the land to hoe
No meet and greet of outer woe

My wise will rise from high and low
My earth will girth from head to toe
My wind daughter will always blow

The lean must wean; power must grow
The peace will feast with bison show
The lineage sure, our tribes do know

The words of a woman chief...

Good-bye?

"I'll see you soon," with tissue held

we with strength put tears aside
take the yoke however wide
and carry that in quickest stride

"I'll see you soon," not good-bye

reaches hopeful as it should
yet humbly stated if you would
gives some cheer when understood

and should you feel this mutual need
it brings a blessing inward creed
in the common simple deed

"I'll see you soon"

The Visit

Simple text
On the road
She is near
Unlock door
Open, close
Boots aside
Sit or spread
Couch is warm
Senses filled
Tea is green
Light is dim
Darkness sets
Soon to leave
Scarf is left
Tomorrow
Another text

Boomerang

We were chatting on a starless porch with no family about and he posed, "Do you believe the phrase 'like father/like A' or 'like mother/like B' is applicable to someone like me?"

Not desiring the debate, as the night was late, I said, "A solid question for a different day..." And so maneuvered some delay.

Yet, it would challenge me, the opportunity unaddressed, with examining the reactive of roles with give and tiff...every time she is angry at her significant other that emotion could fall upon the head of father or mother.

Dang! Like a boomerang!

However, if she is pleased by a kind or exceptional act, and thinks the parents have brought up or raised a marvelous son, that compliment is sweeter than actual fact.

Wow! It's good to be a mother!

All Occasions

She has a flair that's very rare
to care for high and low or not

It cast a lure with equal spur
fixing venue full secure

A likely meet flows and grows
finessed with favored shows

This stellar site moves a deal
with free and strong appeal

A give n' take steels the fake
of funding by a shake

To prove fair, that says I care
for high and low or not

In all occasions, then and now,
inclusive true is sought

Generations

The Queen Crown was
once stored in a cabinet,
a chipped, royal design
with mother's firm
don't touch!

The antique pedestal
for festive dessert
was handed down
with excess years of
caution.

Eventually,
the heirloom
did claim its display,
and was used
often!

A Different Way

"I love you," said little Dan. Then off he ran.
"I love you," said little Ann. "I'll help, I certainly can."
Those verses should have brought me humor, or delight,
yet its replay threatened...
If I run, do I love less? If I work, do I love more?
I couldn't ask, because, she died,
and no one spoke — of her.

But to survive, I ignored them all and took to reading
and that was misunderstood, and it defined me —
a lazy, selfish child, who should be sent off to labor;
and in the thirties, such work was accepted.

After four years of transformation, or so believed,
my relatives moved me upper state
for an advanced education, and then a career;
with marriage and children to follow — yet I grieved.

The past was sad and confusing, until
A powerful message knocked me over:
"When weak, we are strong." His Way.
Therefore, in weakness, I may not work or do
But I can always love, and be loved.
And so to you somewhere, I finally say,
"It's His Way!"

Heat

Seven diverse people
Splintering
You pick, you choose
First round, you lose
That's foreboding
Six diverse people
Seething
You open the door
It's rot to the core
No, it's burning
Five diverse people
Shouting
Foundation deep
Swearing to reap
Be it deadening
Four diverse people
Scrawling
You can, you dare
Inform or care
Yet still conflicting
Three people
Finite
Fervor
Firestorm
Falling
Two people
Then one

An Example of Love

It was you and simplicity
Then something was lost

When they were older
You turned to grandkids
And great grandkids
But they grew up too

Simple can't be boxed in
These efforts are futile
To doubt is downward
Not just now, but after

It's important to release
Acknowledge the adults

Love will never succeed
Until you approach life
With less control and
Something expansive

Today

Fourteen and facing
The problem of flight
Within the climax
Of wrong and right

Telegram sent
Includes the line
"Please, please, sister,
I need some time"

Her one-way route
In choice of no gain
For, not against,
Delaying the strain

Her hindsight voids
Our tomorrow
As if today
Can mark a Jane Doe

Walls

I'm the red brick
All proud outside
Yet acts within
 Doom, and divide

My mortared self
Holds mighty brawls
Of hell and beer
And hefty galls

But with this wear
My cracks grow wide
And they'll mark me
Less strong outside

Who Am I?

You guys out there
The use it or lose it

That one, this one
Mean or meek
Hot or cold
Up and down

But who am I

That girl, this girl
Smart and quick
In between
On the ground

You guys out there
The use it or lose it

That one, this one
Talk or take
With him, with her
Any round

You guys out there
Time to grow up

To Be A Saint

If only I had the courage
of Mother Teresa
to be the leper, to be the cripple,
to be the poor, to be the abandoned,
to be anyone in severe pain;
to take on all this to relieve the other.

I have no courage for this prayer!

I remain a coward,
unless it is my child, and
to that I would hope
to suffer and brave their torment,
to take and bear their pain,
to adapt with great forbearance.

Is this why we are God's children?

Not of the World

To be in the world, and not of the world,
is to witness in deed
and voice
how to participate
and not condone;
and yet it challenges
the way we compromise
and regard pleasure and absorb delight,
and somehow,
still center
on the spiritual.

Timidly, we witness,
not because we fear separation
from the world, our world —
where our love for one another
often exceeds our love for the Supreme —
rather, just because.

The Cross

Journey now
Aloneness harsh
Empty calls
Food is sparse
Yellow skin
My bones ache
I am thin,
With no intake
Yet ordained
In this stage
To know the cross
With no rage

Don't ask how

Just Once

Leave her alone
Alone with me
Leave her guiltless
Beside me
Love and honor
Choose me

Leave her alone
Alone with me
Leave her precious
Oil on me
Grace and goodness
Touch me

Leave her alone
Alone with me
Leave her caress
To anoint me
For
This night

Utopia

Children loved
with hope and sustenance

Daughters graced
with unbiased status

Sons parented
through mutual respect

Sisters blessed
with equal rights

Brothers expanded
by compromise

Communities sustained
with outreach

Nations recognized
for benevolence

A world viewed
with human dignity

Universe
preserved

A Future

The earth will heal

> *Because*

You took a stand

> *Because*

Of waste not, want not

> *Because*

You saved nature

> *Because*

The earth was honored

> *Because*

Greed diminished

> *Because*

Equal mattered

> *Because*

Survivors believed

My Gut Feeling

Is it a brazen excuse
When reasoning resist
Is it a coward's reply
When truth takes to hiding
Is it a biting answer
When the brief cuts corners
Is it a rapid release
When impatience pulls weight
Is it a brain
When effort fails

Gut spoken or
Mind-boggling

Again

My words are now ignored; and I am
trampled upon
as digging eyes hoe me down

Yet under this cloddy look, I shall
sprout again
and re-emerge cultivated,
a hybrid

Then eyes will slide past the tilled
past to present
to regard
my altered freedom

Again.

For Discussion Group:

Some poems are simple, some are complex; the readers are encouraged to discuss the poem on the back cover:

I AM

**He says the body and mind are nothing,
only I AM is consciousness.**

**Dissect him; all organs are found;
but I AM is present—it is timeless.**

**Sight, touch, taste, hearing, smell—
parts of body and mind—or I AM.**

Is this the last romance, or is it love?

A discussion group may want to consider "romance" or being romantic as feeling (through sight, touch, taste, hearing, smell), but even then, at a higher level, romance relates to self-realization or enlightenment or an awakening. Certainly among several of the world religions, releasing of feelings (through meditation) helps center the human mind on something spiritual, or even on "nothingness."

And so the conclusion could be: by emptying ourselves, we actually move toward the highest consciousness of I AM, and may be filled with love.

As this discussion proceeds, more challenging thoughts and ideas may unfold!

Look at this straightforward method of examining words:

Begin with romance, and consider the <u>atypical</u> definition as "an extravagant falsehood."

Now define extravagant as "excessive or unrestrained."

Then consider falsehood as "lacking fact or lacking truth."

So in being not restricted with lack of fact or truth, consider "He says the body and mind are nothing, only I AM is consciousness." This may lead to discussion about the abstract of I AM. Is it consciousness?

Science can "dissect him" or analyze critically the physical body, the sensory organ system, but can we analyze consciousness? The poet says I AM is present and it is timeless. (Quantum physics has particular views about time; if one considers fifth dimension, or considers quantum physics, then the interpretation may be deeper). More important, can I AM exist without the body and mind?

Consider I AM as entering, or not entering, the body and mind by the will of a supernatural spirit. If "entering" is possible, does this separate humans from all other life forms in evolution?

We understand mind as a realm where we interpret information, creating our perceptions of the world, and then, we consider its interconnection to the sensory organ system (sight, touch, taste, hearing and smell), seeing these senses as the transducers from the physical world to the realm of mind. So then, what about I AM?

If I AM does not exist, then a supernatural spirit interpretation is the "last romance," or the last extravagant falsehood. But if it does exist, we may define I AM consciousness as love. (Or agape at the highest level — a self-sacrificing unconditional love). These ideas may morph into controversial or complicated discussions.

Whether a group discussion or a chosen quiet read, ultimately, the reader may ask, "Why does the poet use the word "romance" when "falsehood" is a more simple interpretational approach? Perhaps romance (or romantic) demands attention, feels puzzling, and then pushes toward diverse exploration.

www.ingramcontent.com/pod-product-compliance
Lightning Source LLC
Chambersburg PA
CBHW032044290426
44110CB00012B/939